MW00695665

Contents

Introduction

Welcome to the *Psychic Awakening Journal*. I am so happy that you found your way here, and I am delighted to be your guide as you open up to your psychic abilities.

If you are still wondering whether you are psychic, the answer is yes! You are. And actually, everyone is. Psychic ability is a lot like athletic ability: everyone has some, and we can all actualize our potential if we work at it. Just like if you wanted to get physically fit, eventually you would have to put down the books about working out and show up in the gym. Psychic ability is just like a muscle that needs regular workouts to grow.

It takes two things to maximize our psychic skills: knowledge and practice. This prompted journal is all about the practice. One of the very first things I ask my psychic students to do is to get a journal and label it "Psychic Journal." With this journal, I am so thrilled to have created the perfect one, just for you.

Journaling our psychic experiences is important because even the most significant psychic experience can have an ephemeral quality to it. We forget our experiences very easily. If you experience a psychic hit on a Monday and don't write it down, by the time it happens a few days later, you might easily have forgotten your earlier psychic impression. In the twenty-plus years that I have been teaching psychic development classes, I have found that this one thing is often the key to realizing how psychic we already are. And since what we put our attention on grows, having a dedicated journal practice is a sure way to increase psychic abilities.

How to Use This Journal

To get the most out of your journal experience, I recommend setting aside about twenty minutes a day to do the exercises and journal about them. Go through the prompts and exercises and do one a day, writing down what comes to you. It doesn't have to be every day, but committing to a regular practice will get you there quicker, just like it would if you were going to the gym. Or better yet, use your intuition to guide you through this process and do as much or as little as you feel drawn to. There may be days when your psychic abilities are really on and you want to move through some new territory quickly. On other days, you may just feel the need to take a break. Pacing yourself is important as you are building new psychic muscles; you want to go along at a pace that creates new habits and gives you the results you are looking for without getting burned-out and fatigued along the way.

In the spirit of using your intuition with this journal, I also invite you to skip around the journal and engage in the exercises that you feel pulled to in the moment. See what happens if you set an intention like *What do I need to know right now?* and then let the journal fall open at random and play with whatever exercise you land on.

If you appreciate a more structured approach, you may do very well with going through the process in the order it is presented.

Then use the pages at the end of this book to record any psychic or intuitive impressions that you experience throughout the day. These pages offer space for you to:

◆ Record your dreams—tips on how to do this coming right up!

◆ Record your daily oracle or tarot card pulls.

◆ Write down all your hunches, nudges, and intuitive impressions.

◆ Note down signs and omens, like repeating "angel numbers," feathers or coins you find, or songs you hear on the radio that you know are signs for you.

- ✦ Record your first impressions of people, places, and situations.

- ✦ Observe any time you might sense the presence of a spirit around you.

Write any and all psychic impressions, and you will be amazed by how psychic you already are.

I know that as you are guided by inspirational daily prompts and room to record psychic impressions, using this psychic journal will help you discover, trust, and strengthen your psychic awareness step-by-step and day-by-day.

A Note About Me

I knew about my psychic gifts early on, but back when I was a child, there were no psychics on TV, no books or classes or even psychic teachers. I had to figure it all out the hard way. I started working as a psychic when I was nineteen years old and have been doing so ever since. My mission in life is to help train psychics, healers, and empaths to fully step into their gifts because I think the world needs all the healers it can get, now more than ever.

If you want to go deeper into the possibilities of being a healer and how to blend that with your psychic abilities, then check out my book *The Art of Psychic Reiki*. If you feel you might be an empath and are looking for full training on how to master your empath abilities, then my book *Energy Healing for Empaths* is for you. And if you want a deep dive and the backstory on the psychic worlds, my book *Awakening Your Psychic Abilities* is a fantastic supplement to this journal.

These are all tools I wish I had when I was trying to figure out how to fully open my psychic abilities and use them to help myself and other people too. I am thrilled to bring this information to you to help you open and explore with ease and grace. And to have some fun doing it.

Let's begin!

1

Setting Your Intention

Our intentions really matter, and deciding and then declaring your intention can help set the container for this journal, assist you in sticking with it, and begin to draw that future toward you. Intention setting is powerful stuff!

The Magic Wand Exercise

Imagine that you had a magic wand and you could wave it over your life. How would you imagine that letting yourself be fully psychic and intuitive would help you be your best self? Consider the following and write down what comes to you:

Would you like to use your newfound psychic skills to navigate your own life and be in the right place at the right time? When was the last time that happened?

Does having full access to your psychic insights help you discover your life's purpose? How could it help you in your current work life?

_____

_____

_____

_____

_____

_____

Would fully activating your psychic potential help you achieve some of your dreams, perhaps to meet your soulmate, or find the right home or work for yourself?

_____

_____

_____

_____

_____

_____

Maybe you want to use your psychic gifts to help other people. Who would you want to help, and how would you want to help them?

> I would like to
> help others:
> — I want to fully
> unlock all my
> psychic gifts as
> a psychic, medium,
> + healer
> I want to explore
> clairaudience

Do you have a desire to fully unlock your psychic potential and explore what your gifts really are? Maybe you even want to become a professional psychic and live your life as a healer. What are the gifts you want to explore?

Let your imagination run loose as you write a vision for your best self. Finish this sentence: If I could fully master my psychic ability, I would be so thrilled and happy to use it for these things:

Set Your Intention

Contemplate what came up for you in the Magic Wand Exercise and craft that into an intention for your journal experience.

I want to fully explore my psychic potential so I can: _____

_____

_____

_____

_____

_____

_____

_____ .

2

Releasing Fear

Maybe you are so ready to open up your psychic abilities that you have no fear or resistance at all. If that is true, then congratulations! On the other hand, you may need to take a look at any fears or blocks you have about being psychic. You might need to clear out the obstacles to your psychic opening.

In order to open up, sometimes we need to release fear. Many people are nervous about being psychic and are holding onto those fears, which can block their opening. Some of us have had scary experiences in the past or are having to sort through the beliefs about what being psychic means that we picked up from our families and religious communities. Let's open up those beliefs and experiences and bring them into the light of day so we can examine and release them.

Looking at Your Fears and Concerns

Do you have any fear about opening up to your psychic abilities? Do you relate to any of the following? Check the ones that apply to you.

- ◯ People will think I am crazy. They put people who see spirits and hear voices in mental hospitals, right?

- ◯ I might actually go crazy. Psychic experiences make me feel unhinged. I just want to be normal.

- ◯ If I open up, I will experience bad and scary things that I can't control and maybe even attract more of them to me.

- ◯ You have to be special to be psychic. I am just ordinary!

- ◯ I worry people will make fun of me and think it's a big joke or a scam.

- ◯ Everyone knows psychics are evil and the gifts come from the devil.

Did I miss any of yours? Let's bring them all into the light of day. Write down any other fears here.

_____

_____

_____

_____

Clearing Past Fears

Let's explore where those fears came from.

Did you have bad experiences as a child? Let's bring those memories into the light of day. Record here any negative, scary, or unsettling psychic experiences that you have had anytime in your life.

What did your family believe about psychic experiences? Were such experiences tolerated, or were they feared and shut down? Check the statement that fits for you.

◯ My family was totally cool with my psychic experiences and really encouraged and supported me.

◯ They were pretty supportive but had no idea how to help me or explain what was happening.

◯ They were total nonbelievers and told me that I was making it all up.

◯ They were terrified of the whole idea and ready to throw holy water on me.

How did their beliefs and attitudes about psychic phenomena impact you? Where you allowed to explore the psychic worlds, or did you have to shut it down? List three ways this impacted you.

1. _____

2. _____

3. _____

What about your religion, faith tradition, and other communities? Many of us come from families whose religious beliefs strongly impacted whether we were allowed to explore our psychic gifts or not. What were the messages your religious upbringing taught you about people with psychic abilities? Check the ones your communities taught you.

○ Psychic skills are forbidden and clearly come from the devil, so I had to hide what I was experiencing.

○ Only priests, pastors, imams, or other religious leaders are allowed to have these experiences, not regular people.

○ Only science is real, so all psychics are scammers and charlatans.

○ All of these gifts, including mine, come from divine sources.

Are there any other beliefs you have about psychics that you are ready to let go of? Write down any negative beliefs about psychics here.

_____

_____

_____

_____

_____

_____

_____

Are you ready to let those go and start with a clean slate?

◯ Yes   ◯ No

If you checked no, go back through the "Looking at Your Fears and Concerns" and "Clearing Past Fears" sections above and see if there is anything else to uncover. What else do you need to do to let go of your fears and move forward?

_____

_____

_____

_____

_____

_____

If you are a yes, let's continue!

Who Would You Be
Without Those Fears?

What would you do and who would you be if you released those fears and felt 100 percent comfortable with your gifts? Take a moment to imagine your life if you were totally tapped into your gifts right now and felt free to express your psychic gifts fully.

Make a list of all the things that you would use your gifts for.

1. _____

2. _____

3. _____

4. _____

5. _____

3

Preparing to Open Up

Now that you have cleared out all of your fears and concerns, let's take a look at a few other potential obstacles that can block your ability to open your psychic abilities. Learning to normalize psychic experiences is a great step as well as making sure that you are not blocking the guidance you are receiving because you simply don't want to hear the message.

It's Normal!

Most of the time, being psychic is a very normal everyday occurrence. Check the box for each of the following questions that you would answer yes to.

- ◯ Have you ever known that the phone was going to ring before it did?

- ◯ Have you ever thought, *I have a bad/good feeling about this,* right before something happened?

- ◯ Have you ever had a dream or a daydream that came true?

- ◯ Do you experience hunches or nudges that allow you to be at the right place at the right time?

- ◯ Have you ever heard a little voice inside your head that gives you good advice when you need it?

- ◯ Do you ever see things out of the corner of your eyes, and when you look closer, nothing is there?

If you have had any of these, congratulations! You have had a psychic experience!

Write more about any psychic experiences that stand out in your mind. Finish this sentence: This is the psychic experience that stands out the most in my mind:

Are You Rejecting Your Messages?

Sometimes we shut down our messages because we don't actually want to hear what our guidance tells us. Our wisest self may be nudging us to move out of our comfort zone and make some changes in our lives or be asking us to confront difficult and painful things that need attending to.

Is there inner guidance that you are avoiding right now?

_____

_____

_____

_____

Why are you avoiding it?

_____

_____

_____

_____

_____

What do you think would happen if you listened to and acted on this guidance?

_____

_____

_____

_____

_____

Are you ready to let that go and open up?

◯ Yes ◯ No

If you answered no, write about what you need in order to be ready.

_____

_____

_____

_____

_____

_____

_____

Declaration

Write down your declaration that you are ready to open up fully to your psychic abilities right now.

"I declare that I am awakening my psychic abilities right now!"

Or use your own words.

_____

_____

_____

_____

Describe how that felt.

_____

_____

_____

_____

_____

_____

_____

4

Paying Attention to the Whispers

A big part of opening up our psychic ability is taking time to tune in and listen. We need to find that quiet, open, receptive time when our being is still and we are open to receiving our guidance. Here are some great tips and exercises to help you do just that.

Alpha Activities

When we drop into the "alpha" brain wave, we are the most open and receptive to intuition and creativity. This happens naturally when we do repetitive activities that don't require much active thought. Have you noticed that you get your best psychic hits while you are doing one of these things? Check any activities that have brought on a psychic experience.

- ◯ Driving, especially on a familiar route
- ◯ Taking a shower
- ◯ Doing dishes or folding laundry
- ◯ Walking or yoga
- ◯ Mowing the lawn

What are your favorite alpha activities?

_____

_____

_____

_____

_____

_____

The next time you are engaged in one of your alpha activities, really pay attention to any psychic impressions that you have. Record them here.

Alpha Practice

Ask yourself a question about something you need some insight on in your life. Write your question down here.

_____

_____

_____

_____

Now go do one of your favorite alpha activities and let the question go, but pay attention to any insights that arise during your activity. Notice how you feel and any thoughts, inspirations, or aha moments that you have during your alpha activity. Record your insights here.

_____

_____

_____

_____

_____

_____

_____

Tuning In Meditation

Find a place to sit quietly and take a few centering breaths. Begin to open your awareness to your psychic impressions. Try writing or speaking aloud the affirmation *I am open to receiving guidance now.* You can ask a specific question or something more general, like "What do I need to know right now?" Tune in to how you feel, what you feel in your body, any words that pop into your head, and images that you might see. Reflect on what you received and jot it down here.

The Truth Signal

Chances are good that your body will experience a very clear sensation when you hear the truth and get a real psychic hit. For some people, it's tears or shivers or gooseflesh. What do you think yours is? List any bodily sensations that you experience during your psychic impressions here.

If you are not sure, spend a few days observing yourself. Once you know what the sensation is for you, pay close attention to what is happening the next time you feel it. What did you discover? Record your body sensations here.

Hunches and Nudges

Have you ever felt a hunch about something or a little nudge that comes across as an impulse to do something outside your normal routine? What happened when you followed this? Write down three times you can remember this happening and what came out of it.

1. _____

_____

_____

_____

2. _____

_____

_____

_____

3. _____

_____

_____

_____

Opening Up Your Intuition

Your intuition is a combination of several psychic senses working together. We experience this as a trifecta of psychic impressions that come through our bodies, our feelings, and our gut sense of knowing. Let's take an example that we can all relate to, and see if you can pinpoint how your intuition has been showing up to support you all along. Can you remember a time when you met someone for the first time and had either a very strong negative or positive reaction?

I remember! It happened when I met: _____

How did your body react when you met that person? Did it open and relax or tighten up? Complete these sentences:

When I first met _____, I felt the sensation

of _____ in this part of my

body _____. And I knew right away that meant

_____.

What did your emotions tell you about this meeting? Maybe you felt very comfortable with the person right away or you got an instant bad vibe. List three emotions that you felt at this first meeting.

1. _____

2. _____

3. _____

What was your gut knowing about this person? We experience this as *I am not sure how I know; I just know*. To explore this, finish this sentence:

This is what I knew right away about that person:

_____

_____

_____

_____

_____

_____

_____

As you got to know that person over time, was your first, intuitive impression correct?

Circle one: 100% correct Mostly correct I was way off the mark

The Wisdom of Your Belly Meditation

Your belly is wise and usually knows what's really going on in any situation that you are in. Close your eyes and take a few breaths.

1. Drop your breath and awareness into your belly and ask it to tell you something that you need to know right now. Or think of a situation you are in that is confusing to you.

2. Notice if your belly feels tight and stressed or loose and relaxed. Our bellies will relax and feel loose and soft when we are safe and headed in the right direction. And they will tense up and feel sick and maybe even queasy when we are headed in the wrong direction.

3. Ask your belly to show the answer to a specific question or just ask if there is anything in general that you need to know.

Journal about your experience here.

From now on, try to notice what is happening in your belly. If it's tight and stressed, figure out why. You can use this like a rudder on a ship and steer toward things that make your belly loose and happy and away from things that keep it tight.

Feeling It in Your Bones

Let your bones help you decide your path or notice what is really happening in each moment. Our bodies never lie and always know what's really going on. Close your eyes for a moment and just feel your bones. Try breathing into your bones; they are like antennae that we can tune in to.

What are you feeling in your bones right now?

What have you felt in your bones lately?

Using a Pendulum

Pendulums are very useful for learning to trust our psychic impressions. We can get a clear yes, no, or I-don't-know answer from them that can help us confirm or deny our psychic hits. You can get a fancy crystal pendulum or use a safety pin on a string. Set your elbow on a table and hold the string between your thumb and forefinger. First, you need to know the pendulum's language. Ask your pendulum to show you what a "yes" answer looks like and what a "no" answer looks like so you know what the pendulum's response means when you ask a question. You also need to include an "I don't know" option because pendulums don't know everything! Record or draw the pendulum's movements here.

"Yes" looks like this:

"No" looks like this:

"I don't know" looks like this:

Next time you get a psychic hit that you are not totally confident about, you can use your pendulum to confirm or deny that you were right. Remember to keep your questions in a simple yes-no format ("Was that really an angel that I sensed in my room last night?") and you have a powerful way to learn to trust your psychic hits.

Try it out and record your results here.

5

Staying Grounded and Centered

Being grounded means being in your body, connected to the earth, and keeping your mind in the present moment. It's super important to stay grounded as you open up psychically. It's step one of your energy-hygiene practices and should be done in preparation for psychic activity and anytime you feel spacy.

Grounding Checklist

Here are some good ways to ground. Check the ones that you know work for you.

- ◯ Sitting on the earth or with your back to a tree
- ◯ Standing bare feet on the ground
- ◯ Light exercise, like yoga or walking
- ◯ Heavy exercise, like running and weight lifting
- ◯ Eating mindfully and taking good care of your body
- ◯ Drinking water with a little salt or electrolytes in it
- ◯ Breathing deeply and setting the intention to be more grounded

Write down any other grounding techniques that you know work for you.

_____

_____

_____

_____

_____

_____

Learning to Center

Centering means bringing your energy home to yourself. We get scattered out of ourselves as we move about the world, and in order to do psychic work safely, we must always begin and end by coming home to ourselves.

Spend a moment to journal about what throws you off your center and how being off-center makes you feel.

Centering Practice

Close your eyes and take a breath. Put your hand on the part of you that feels like the place where your essence resides in your body. Don't think about it too much, just put your hand on your body. This is your center. Take a deep breath and breathe yourself back into your center.

Circle the part(s) of you that feels like your center.

What did you feel like before you were centered?

And after?

Breathing into Your Tailbone

This is a fantastic way to ground yourself. Take a deep breath into your tailbone. Breathe all the way from the top of your head down your spine and let your breath land in your tailbone. Now imagine that your tailbone is extending down through the chair you are in, through the layers of the building, and down deep into the earth. Let it go as deep and wide as you can. This is called a *grounding cord*, and you can visualize it anytime you need grounding.

Draw a picture of what the grounding cord looked or felt like to you.

Roots Down

Push your feet into the floor and imagine that there are roots coming out of your feet. Let those roots go deep down into the earth. See what happens if you spread them out wide all the way around you.

How did you feel before you put the roots down?

_____

_____

_____

_____

_____

How did you feel afterward?

_____

_____

_____

_____

_____

Grounding with a Tree

Find a tree somewhere that you can sit next to. Put your back against the trunk of the tree. Take a few breaths and imagine that your own grounding cord and roots are traveling down into the earth with the tree's roots. Now imagine that your head is up in the branches of the tree. This is a great way to both ground and also open up your psychic experiences.

Journal about your experience here.

6

Energy Clearing

Good psychic hygiene is essential to doing psychic work. Psychic energy can accumulate and clog up your psychic senses if you don't clear it out on a regular basis. Other people's emotions, thoughts, and sensations can leave an energy residue in our own energy field and in our environments that we need to clean out so we can receive clear messages ourselves. Being in psychically chaotic situations can also drain your energy if you don't know how to clear and protect yourself. Here are some ways to recognize when you need to cleanse your energy and some powerful ways to clear out any residual energy that you might pick up.

What Drains You?

Look back at your last few weeks and consider the people, places, and situations that you were in that really drained you. Notice who and what made you feel tired, cranky, and drained of your energy.

○ Work or school

○ At home or with family

○ When you are out shopping and running errands

○ Social situations, like parties, restaurants, or concerts

○ Are there certain people who always drain you?

Did I miss any? Write your own here.

_____

_____

_____

_____

_____

Body Scan

How do you know that your energy is being drained or you have picked up negative energy? Here is a quick and easy way to scan your whole system so you can find the energy leaks and any negative vibes that you picked up from other people, places, or situations.

Close your eyes and take a few breaths down your spine to bring yourself into the present moment. Tune in to your body, and using your attention and intention, scan your body from your head to your toes and notice any place that feels tight, restricted, or in pain. Record what you discovered in your body here.

_____

_____

_____

_____

Now breathe some white into those body parts and clear out any residual energy on your exhale. How does your body feel now? Write about any changes you noticed here.

_____

_____

_____

_____

Scanning Your Emotions

Now try scanning your emotions. Take a few breaths to help you get grounded and turn your attention to your thoughts and feelings. Notice what feelings are right on the surface. Are any lurking below the surface that need to be acknowledged? Emotions often clear when we validate and acknowledge them. Try breathing some white light into wherever you are feeling your emotions and feel love and appreciation for your emotions.

Journal about that experience here.

Mind Clearing

Our thoughts can also be impacted when we are exposed to the chaotic energy of other people and the world. It can create a spiral of negative or chaotic thinking inside of us too, and we can feel like our thoughts are spinning.

Take a few grounding and centering breaths and close your eyes. Tune in to your thoughts and just observe them without judgment. Are they calm and clear, jumbled and spinning out of control, or somewhere in between?

Finish the sentence:

I am thinking about _____

_____, and I notice that my thoughts are

_____

_____

_____.

Now close your eyes again and bring your attention up into your mind. Imagine a ball of light forming in the center of your head, and on the next exhale, breathe that light out through your head like a wave. Hold a gentle intention to clear your thoughts and let this wave of light move through your head until your thoughts feel clear.

Journal about what that was like for you.

Quick Clearing Breath

Take a deep breath and breathe all the way down to your tailbone to fully ground yourself. If you are feeling any tightness, pain, or emotion in your system, then direct your breath to that spot. Now breathe out with a quick breath making a little whooshing sound with your exhale to release any residual energy you are feeling.

How did it feel and what was released?

The Compost Bin

Write down everything here that you would like to clear from you right now. This can be other people's energy, the residue you picked up from your surroundings, or any of your own energy, thoughts, or feelings that are not serving you. Bin them now.

Waterfall of Light Clearing Meditation

Take one breath to center yourself and one breath into your tailbone to ground yourself. Imagine you are standing under a beautiful waterfall of light that is falling all around you. This beautiful light is washing away any negativity and energy residue, leaving you squeaky clean.

What was that like? How did you feel before you did that, and how did you feel afterward? Write about your experience here.

Salt Clearing and Bath or Shower Oracle

This is a great combination for energy clearing.

Step 1: Cleanse your energy. When you need a deep energy clean, try either a salt bath or shower. Any kind of salt will do. Put some bath salts in your tub before your bath and set an intention to have it cleanse you of any energy you picked up that doesn't belong to you. You can make a scrub with salt for your shower. I make a super simple shower salt scrub by using coconut oil, sea salt, and whatever essential oils I have on hand. Clearing ourselves before we ask a question will yield "cleaner" results.

Step 2: Ask a question. Now that your energy is clear and squeaky clean, ask a question that you need an answer to and then just let your mind and attention drift, but pay attention to any aha moments that you have. Pay attention to any images, thoughts, feelings, or knowings that might arise as you are relaxing in the tub or shower. Try journaling in your tub!

What question did you ask?

How did the salt clearing feel? Finish this sentence: I let go of these thoughts, feelings, and body sensations:

_____

_____

_____

_____

_____

_____

Finish this sentence: This is the insight I received about my question:

_____

_____

_____

_____

_____

_____

_____

_____

7

Psychic Protection

Psychic protection is another vital part of maintaining good psychic hygiene. Psychic protection is all about learning to set boundaries. It's a difficult skill for many sensitives to master, but the good news is that once we learn how to set a boundary, it works in all the situations that we might find ourselves. For the most part, we are protecting ourselves from the energy of other people, but we are also impacted by the environments we are in and sometimes spiritual energy too. Having good energetic and psychic boundaries means you can continue to open psychically and still be safe. Here are some easy but powerful ways to level up your psychic protection.

Boundaries

Your boundaries are important, and you have the right to say no and set boundaries about whom you allow into your psychic space. Are you good at setting boundaries, or do you need some work on that? Which statement is true for you?

○ I set boundaries like a boss; nothing gets in without my express permission.

○ I am good with boundaries in some situations but really bad in other situations.

○ It's really hard for me to set boundaries, but I know I should. I just need to learn how to!

○ I have very weak boundaries and am always getting invaded by everyone and everything.

○ Boundary—what's that?? I have no idea what this really means or how to do it.

Saying No

Boundaries are really about knowing when and how to say yes or no to people and situations. As sensitives, it's often really difficult to say no to people or to even tell when we need to say no. Here are some things to consider.

What were the rules in your family about saying no? Was saying no something parents could say but children couldn't? Were you allowed to say no as a child?

_____

_____

_____

How easy is it for you to say no now?

_____

_____

_____

Is there anyone in your life whom you feel you can never say no to? List them here.

1. _____

2. _____

3. _____

Resentment Inventory

If you struggle with even knowing when to say no, try this very illuminating exercise. Resentment is a red flag indicating that you need to reset your boundaries and that you are over-giving in a situation.

List everything in your life that you feel resentful about. It might be certain people in your life or situations, such as in your workplace or family environment.

1. _____

2. _____

3. _____

4. _____

5. _____

6. _____

7. _____

8. _____

9. _____

10. _____

Contemplate your list and consider where and how you need to step back and renegotiate what you are willing to do and how much you are comfortable giving. Brainstorm about that here.

Practice Saying No

Sometimes we need to practice how to say no so it's easier for us. Look into a mirror and practice saying the following statements until you can look yourself in the eyes and say them with a real smile too.

- ✦ No thank you.

- ✦ I would love to help you, but I am overbooked right now.

- ✦ Thank you so much for asking me, but I am unable to do that.

- ✦ I'm flattered you considered me, but unfortunately, I'll have to pass this time.

- ✦ Thank you for thinking of me, but I can't.

Circle the ones that would work for you.

Did I miss any that you already use? Record them here.

_____

_____

_____

_____

_____

Medicine Shield Drawing

This circle represents your boundary. Draw a picture of you on the inside of the circle. Write down everything and everyone you allow inside your boundary. On the outside of the circle, write or draw the experiences and people that are not permitted inside your boundary.

How did it feel to do that?

Did anything come up that surprised you?

Protection Bubble Meditation

Take a breath or two to ground, center, and clear yourself. Now imagine a big bubble of energy around you at about an arm's length out. Notice what color your bubble is and its texture. It's interesting to change the color of your bubble too. For extra protection, try imagining a bubble that has a mirror on the outside, like mirrored sunglasses or tinted windows, with bulletproof glass.

Draw a picture of what your bubble looked like here.

Use this bubble anytime you need psychic protection by imaging and intending that it is in place around you.

8

Opening Your Psychic Senses

Our psychic senses are how we perceive our psychic experiences, and you may have heard about these as your "clairs." Our psychic senses are related to our physical senses, but there is a difference. You might pick up things with your psychic ears and eyes that your physical senses are not perceiving. You may have only one or two of your "clairs" opened up and available to you at present, but with practice, you can open them all. Or you may already have them all open. No psychic sense is better than any of the others, so be open to whatever you experience.

Your Psychic Senses

These are the psychic senses. Which ones are the strongest for you? Or do you have a little bit of all of them?

+ **The body sense.** I feel things in my body and can easily tune in to my body's truth signal and wisdom.

+ *Clairsentience—the feeling sense.* I feel my way through everything. I get emotional reactions to everything, and I am always saying things like, "I have a good/bad feeling about this..."

+ *Claircognizance—the knowing sense.* I don't know how I know, I just know.

+ *Clairaudience—the auditory sense.* I hear that voice in my head all the time!

+ *Clairvoyance—the visual sense.* I see things moving out of the corners of my eyes, have vivid dreams, easily visualize things, and also see things in my mind's eye all the time.

+ *Clairgustance—the tasting sense, and clairalience—the smelling sense.* I can taste and smell when something is not right. I have a great sense of smell, and sometimes I smell things that aren't really there!

Which of these psychic senses do you relate to the most?

Write down a time you experienced a psychic impression. Which of your psychic senses were functioning, and what was that like for you? Journal about it here.

Your Body's Wisdom

Your body always knows what's real and is alert to danger. Take a moment to ground yourself and then tune in to your body to see where you feel your psychic awareness.

+ Does your skin get gooseflesh?

+ Is your belly doing flip-flops?

+ Is your heart feeling tight or happy?

+ Or is there somewhere else you tend to feel your body's wisdom?

Where do you feel things in your body, and what does it feel like? Write about a time when you felt a psychic impression and what that was like for you.

_____

_____

_____

_____

_____

_____

_____

Tuning In to Your Feelings

If you have clairsentience, you feel your way through life. Empaths, this is you! It might come through your emotional states, or you might find yourself saying, "I have a good/bad feeling about that..."

Close your eyes for a minute and draw your breath and your attention to your lower belly. Open up the awareness of your feeling self and ask if there are any messages for you right now, or try asking a direct question about something and record your experience here.

Deep Knowing

Your inner knowing is almost always right and is especially good at summing up people right away. Think about one time that you have said, "I knew that was going to happen..." and write about it here.

_____

_____

_____

_____

_____

Have you ever had that deep inner knowing about a person and been right? How did you know, and what happened? Record that experience here.

_____

_____

_____

_____

_____

_____

_____

Pay attention the next time you meet someone new. Let your gut, your inner knowing, inform you about that person, and record your impressions here.

That Little Voice Inside Your Head

Sometimes the voice in your head is actually your inner guidance or even one of your spirit guides. To find the voice of your inner guidance, try this.

1. Take a few breaths to center, ground, and clear yourself.

2. Consider something that you would like an answer to and write it down here.

_____

_____

_____

3. Now and turn your attention inward and tune in to the voice in your head. Write the answer here; don't overthink it, just write.

_____

_____

_____

_____

_____

_____

4. Great job! Now that you know how to do this, pay careful attention to that little voice in your head and write down any pearls of wisdom.

Encouraging Clairvoyance

Our inner sight can provide fantastic psychic information for us. Most of the time, it's like having a little daydream or seeing something in your mind's eye. Giving the eyes something to focus on helps a lot.

Ask yourself a question or even ask, "What do I need to know right now?" and then gaze at something that is off in the distance a little bit and let your eyes go slightly out of focus. Let your mind wander a bit and see what comes to you. Try one of the following focus points.

+ Gaze at the clouds moving by.

+ Soft-focus your eyes on the treetops moving in the wind or watch the grass grow.

+ Look at fire flickering in a fireplace, a bonfire, or a candle flame.

+ Gaze at moving water.

Journal about what you experienced here.

Tasting and Smelling

Smell is the sense most linked to our memory and therefore can really evoke the spirits of loved ones who have passed on. Have you ever smelled someone's perfume or cologne or even caught the whiff of cooking or tobacco smoke when there was no one there?

Do any of your loved ones who have passed on have a signature smell like that? Have you ever noticed smelling it? Or do you remember the taste of something that reminded you of them? List any times you can recall this happening here.

9

Signs, Omens, and Synchronicities

Signs, omens, and synchronicities are confirmation that our psychic guidance is real and on point. They are like signposts along the way, letting us know that we are headed in the right direction. But we do need to pay attention to them and to learn how to interpret what they mean. When you receive psychic guidance, you can ask for a sign to help you confirm that it's right. You might ask for a specific sign, like feathers or pennies, or you can just tune in to the magical happenings around you.

Repeating Numbers

If you have a strong connection to angels, you might be seeing repeating numbers because angels often use number sequences as a way to communicate with us. Do you notice the 11:11 on the clock every day? Those double numbers are often messages from angels; loved ones who have passed on also send us messages through number sequences. These are usually birthday, anniversary, or death day dates.

Do you have numbers or number sequences that have meaning to you? List them here.

_____

What do these numbers mean to you?

_____

_____

_____

The next time you see one that feels significant, write it down here and include what you think the message behind the numbers means to you.

_____

_____

_____

_____

Weather Wisdom

Are you a person who really notices the weather? Many people see signs in the weather, so pay attention to what's happening around you with the weather. It can be as bold as a sudden clap of thunder or as subtle as a gust of wind. Many people find deep meaning in seeing a rainbow or the way light comes through the clouds at the right moment. Can you see shapes in the clouds or sense an ill or favorable wind?

What aspect of the weather speaks to you? Note it down here.

Jot down one occasion when the weather was a powerful omen for you.

The next time it happens, document it here.

Messages from Wildlife

Do you notice hawks, crows, or other types of wildlife everywhere you go? You might have a strong connection to power animals, and if so, they will bring you signs that you are on the right path and that your psychic information is accurate. Let's explore your connection to animals more deeply.

Did you have an animal that you were crazy about as a child, even a mystical animal, like unicorns?

Is there an animal that you love now, and maybe you even have a collection of things representing it, such as butterflies, dolphins, or hummingbirds?

Do you see animals now that mean something to you, perhaps a cardinal that you know is a message from a departed loved one?

Pay close attention and write down one encounter with wildlife that you knew was a sign.

Open a Book

Ask yourself a question and then pick up a book at random. Take a few centering and grounding breaths. Close your eyes and flip through the pages. Stop at a page and then plop your finger on the page. Read the sentence that your finger landed on and record it here.

Did it make sense and answer your question or at least give you something to think about? What did that mean to you? Contemplate the meaning and document it here.

Music Shuffle

Try the same exercise, but with music. Ask a question, such as "What do I need to know today?" and hit shuffle on your playlist or spin your car radio to scan mode and see what comes up. Many people receive messages from loved ones on the other side through music. Pay attention to the music that is playing in stores when you walk in, on elevators, or that you hear driving by in cars. There are messages in the music especially if you are clairaudient.

Write down your question here.

_____

_____

_____

What song came up when you shuffled your playlist or turned on the radio?

_____

_____

What did that mean to you? Describe it here.

_____

_____

_____

_____

10

Dream Time

Our dreams are chock-full of valuable psychic messages for us. Some come from our own subconscious and higher self, and we often receive messages from our spirit guides and prophetic dreams too. With dreams, we need to learn how to remember them and also how to interpret them. Here are some fantastic ways to tap into this gold mine of psychic information.

Dream Declaration

Write down your commitment to remembering your dreams. This tells your subconscious that you intend to remember your dreams, and you will begin to. Keep this journal by your bed and write down any fragments or snippets of dreams in this journal, and you will begin to remember more and more of them.

Copy this down or come up with your own words for it:

"I declare that I am going to remember my dreams so I can access this valuable psychic information."

Pillow Talk

Right before you go to bed, write down a question that you have about your life on a piece of paper. Put it under your pillow and say your dream declaration out loud. Sleep well!

In the morning record any dreams, feelings, sensations, or memories that happened in your sleep.

The Glass of Water Trick

Bring this journal and a glass of water to bed with you. Once you are settled in bed for the night, take a sip of water and say, "With this sip of water, I am going to remember my dreams and get valuable information about this question in my life." Speak your question out loud and write it down here.

_____

_____

_____

This sends a message to your subconscious, which will work on your question and give you an answer through your dreams.

Record any dreams, feelings, or any little wisp of a dream here.

_____

_____

_____

_____

_____

_____

_____

Dream Interpretation Method 1

Recall any dream that you have had recently. Describe it here.

_____

_____

_____

_____

_____

_____

If everything and everyone in the dream is an aspect of you, what are you trying to tell yourself?

_____

_____

_____

_____

_____

_____

Dream Interpretation Method 2

You can use the same or a different dream. Imagine that everything in the dream is symbolic. What do those symbols mean to you? Maybe the book in your dream means knowledge and the water means emotion. Use a dream dictionary to help if you get stuck; there are plenty of good ones online. Practicing like this will help build your dream interpretation muscles.

Are there recurring images in your dreams?

_____

_____

_____

What do these symbols or images mean to you?

_____

_____

_____

_____

_____

_____

Look up the meanings in a dream dictionary and document them here.

How about images that bring a strong emotional reaction? What were the images and the emotions that they gave you? Note them here.

Resolving Nightmares

Nightmares are usually caused by your subconscious trying to find resolution to a trauma or to help you look at feelings that you are avoiding and to find closure to something that is unresolved. You can do that by cooking up a more satisfying ending to the dream where things are safe, resolved, and happy. Maybe you need to uncover some superpowers, like the ability to fly, create buckets of money on demand, time travel, or have super strength. That is okay; it's all a dream, right?

If you have nightmares or a recurring dream, write it down here.

Do you need superpowers to solve the problem that you are facing in your dreams? If so, what are they?

_____

_____

_____

_____

_____

_____

Now write down an alternate ending where everything feels peaceful, resolved, and settled.

_____

_____

_____

_____

_____

_____

_____

_____

11

The Root Chakra—
I Am Safe

Chakras are the naturally occurring energy centers that govern different aspects of our lives and levels of our consciousness. Everyone has them, whether you know about them or not, and understanding our chakras is a fantastic way for us to learn more about ourselves. All of our chakras are receiving psychic information all the time, so when we learn to open up, clear, and pay attention to our chakras, we can receive a lot of psychic information.

People often completely underestimate the power of the root chakra as a psychic barometer! Truthfully, it is one of the most powerful, accurate, and reliable psychic meters that you have. Because it is connected to your body's psychic sense, it is all about the instinct to survive. The root chakra is the foundation part of your intuition, which includes the lower three chakras, and it will give you constant feedback about whether you are safe or not. The root chakra is red and is located at your tailbone. When it's functioning well, you are grounded, embodied, and aware of your physical surroundings at all times. Let's start by assessing what is happening in your root chakra.

Assessing Your Root Chakra

Take a moment to tune in to your body and breathe all the way down to your tailbone and then down your legs and into your feet. Now ask yourself these questions and record the answers here.

Can you feel your legs and your feet?

_____

Are they warm and full of energy or cold and empty feeling?

_____

Does your body feel safe and secure in your environment?

_____

One a scale of I to 10, how grounded, safe, and secure do you feel in your body? A rating of I is not at all grounded, and 10 is fully and completely grounded. This is how open, accessible and clear your root chakra is.

Circle what feels true to you.

1   2   3   4   5   6   7   8   9   10

Clearing Your Root Chakra

This chakra is blocked by fear, so let's try a clearing exercise. This is best done sitting on the ground outside, but if that's not possible right now, sit anywhere you are comfortable. Take a moment to center and clear yourself and then drop your energy into your tailbone. Imagine your tailbone is like the root of a tree and drop it as deep down into the earth as you can.

On your next inhale, breathe the color red up that root and let it fill up your legs and into your tailbone. Then exhale down any fear that you might be feeling about anything. Do this breathing pattern until you feel calm and your legs feel really loose and heavy.

What fears came up to be released?

How do you feel now that you let those fears go?

How did it feel to release those fears and clear your root chakra?

Listening to Your Body

Take a moment to center and ground yourself. Drop your breath, your energy, and your awareness down to your tailbone. Tune in to your body for a moment and ask it to tell you what it needs.

Does your body feel tight or in pain anywhere? Tune in to that and ask your body to tell you what it needs. Record your answers here.

_____

_____

_____

_____

_____

Do you need to be doing anything to take better care of your body?

_____

_____

_____

_____

_____

Is there something you need to stop doing for your body's well-being?

_____

_____

_____

_____

_____

Can your body tell you anything else that you need to know right now?

_____

_____

_____

_____

_____

Thank your body for all this wisdom and make some time to speak to your body every day. Send your body so much love and appreciation; kiss or pat yourself all over!

Root Chakra Energy Shield

When this chakra is open, it gives excellent psychic protection. Try this exercise when you feel like you need to level up your psychic protection. Take a few breaths to center and ground yourself. Activate your root chakra by breathing into your tailbone and then imagining that you are breathing energy up from the earth right into your tailbone. Now imagine that earth energy surrounding you in a big red bubble. This is a great technique if you feel like you need to prevent psychic attack.

Try it right now and document your experience here.

12

The Navel Chakra— My Feelings Guide Me

Your navel chakra is located just a few inches below your belly button, and it's a bright orange color. It is the center of our emotions, our sexuality, and our passion for living our lives. When we are deeply connected to our pleasure and our emotional states, this chakra acts like a rudder on a boat. We want to steer toward what feels good and makes up happy, and we want to move away from pain and states of emotional unhappiness.

Although this seems like it should be easy, the blocks that we have in this chakra disconnect us from our emotions and our pleasure. Guilt and repression block the intuitive information that we receive from this chakra, and it also holds many of our wounds and traumas. This chakra gives us clairsentience, the feeling psychic sense. If you are an empath, you are going to receive much of your psychic information through your feelings!

Connecting with Your Navel Chakra

Because this chakra is all about your emotions and your pleasure, let's look at how easy that is for you. Consider these statements.

- ✦ I feel all my emotions easily; in fact, I am too sensitive and emotional.

- ✦ I feel rather numb most of the time and have trouble connecting to my emotions.

- ✦ My emotions are very balanced. I am not repressing them or feeling flooded by them either.

- ✦ I let myself feel so much pleasure that it's hard to actually get anything done.

- ✦ Pleasure is for other people. I am going through my life like a machine.

- ✦ I let pleasure guide me, but I can also show up and do what I need to do.

As you consider these statements, are you too emotional, shut down to your emotions, or balanced? Record your answer here.

How about pleasure? Do you let yourself go too far, not far enough, or just right? Write it down here.

Clearing Your Navel Chakra

Take a few breaths to center and ground yourself. Put your hands on your lower belly and imagine a big ball of orange light coming out of your hands and into your lower belly. On your inhale breath, fill your navel chakra with orange light, and on the exhale, release any stuck emotions or energy down the grounding cord and into the earth.

What emotions came up for you as you did that? Really let all your feelings come up and come out here.

How did you feel after you let them all go?

Follow Your Bliss

We don't always let ourselves dream about what we really want and what would make us truly happy. There is deep wisdom and inner guidance in exploring what lights us up. What would make you really happy and blissed out in your life right now? Let yourself dream big and write it down here.

Navel Chakra Guidance

Take a few breaths to center and ground yourself. Put your hands on your lower belly and go back to imaging the orange ball of light coming into your navel chakra.

Ask, "What do I need to know right now?" or ask a specific question that you need some guidance on. Write it down here.

_____

_____

_____

Now relax and tune in to your feelings and emotions. Jot down everything that came up for you here.

_____

_____

_____

_____

_____

_____

_____

13

The Solar Plexus Chakra— I Am Powerful

Your solar plexus chakra is the center of your self-esteem and personal power. It's located right in your solar plexus and is a bright sunshiny yellow. When this chakra is strong and open, we feel powerful. We truly accept ourselves and know how and when to set boundaries. This chakra is blocked by shame, which is a kind of self-rejection. Our solar plexus chakra is constantly giving us accurate data about other people. It's amazing at summing up other people, and this is where our psychic sense of claircognizance comes from. It's that gut knowing that can discern the truth from the lies.

Feeling Your Power

Take a few centering, clearing, and grounding breaths and place your hands on your solar plexus. Imagine bright yellow light coming from your hands into your solar plexus and really breathe, relaxing your diaphragm into some belly breathing if you can. Consider these questions.

On a scale from 1 to 10, how powerful do you feel, where 1 is feeling like a doormat and 10 is feeling like you are a ninja that no one would mess with. Circle where you are today.

1   2   3   4   5   6   7   8   9   10

Are there certain people in your life whom you don't feel powerful around?

_____

_____

_____

What situations do you find yourself in where you have lost your power?

_____

_____

_____

When do you feel at your most powerful?

Clearing Your Solar Plexus Chakra

This is a fun one. Find a place where you can feel free to express yourself. Stand up and stomp your feet, make your hands into fists, and say "No!" as loud as you can. Really throw a no-saying tantrum if you can.

Take a pause, catch your breath, and consider what that was like for you. Was it easy or hard to say no? Did it pour out with some anger, or could you barely squeak out the word? Jot down here what that was like for you.

_____

_____

_____

_____

Now stand up again and put your hands in the air. Say "Yes!" and jump a little if you can. Let your movements and your voice get louder until you feel like you are complete with it.

How was it to say yes? Do you know what you were saying yes to?

_____

_____

_____

Power Statements

Read through these power statements and circle the ones that you feel like you need the most or the ones that really resonate with you. Make a point to say them a few times a day or when you feel you need a power boost.

- ✦ I am strong, confident, and powerful.

- ✦ I will not settle for less than I deserve.

- ✦ I can accomplish great things, and I believe in myself 100 percent.

- ✦ I am enough, just as I am right now.

- ✦ I know my true value and will not take less than that ever.

- ✦ I trust myself to know what is true and right for me.

Write your own here.

The Power of Discernment

Think about a decision that you need to make or a person you know. Put your hand on your solar plexus and send bright yellow energy into that chakra so it is open and strong. What is your gut telling you about that situation or person?

Document it here.

14

The Heart Chakra—
I Love Myself

The heart chakra is where we feel love for ourselves and for other people too. It's the chakra of relationships, and it's located right in the center of our chest and is a brilliant forest-green color. When this chakra is open, we are full of love and compassion for ourselves and for others. It's blocked by unprocessed grief and lack of forgiveness, and so many of us are living with painful broken hearts all the time.

Its psychic superpower is the ability to read what is happening in our relationships. Our hearts understand the subtle dynamics of what is truly going on between people, and our hearts will feel uneasy and unsettled when things are in turmoil. Your heart knows when your people are not okay or a relationship is in jeopardy, even if they are not speaking up about it. And yet the best thing we can do to balance our heart chakra is to love up on ourselves as much as we can.

Feeling Your Heart

Take a moment to center, ground, and clear yourself. Now put your hand on your heart chakra, which is right in the center of your chest. This chakra is connected to your breath, so take some slow, deep breaths. Try breathing in for four counts and exhaling for four counts. Send bright green energy into your heart and just take a moment to feel what you are holding in your heart today.

+ Is your heart open, joyful, and feeling love for you and everyone else?

+ Is it heavy with grief and tears?

+ Is it shut down and cold?

+ Is it bitter, angry, and holding onto hurts from the past?

+ Are you able to love yourself right now?

Take a moment to journal about the experience of feeling your own heart.

Clearing Your Heart Chakra

To clear the heart chakra, we must release grief and begin a cycle of forgiveness. Let's clean it out now.

Confess any grief that you have not expressed right here. Finish this sentence: I am still feeling heartbroken about:

_____

_____

_____

_____

Are you ready to let go of grief and begin to forgive? List the people, including yourself, that you are ready to begin to forgive.

1. _____

2. _____

3. _____

4. _____

5. _____

Congratulations, you have taken some really powerful steps to open your heart!

Love Letter to Yourself

Self-love is a crucial step in opening up our heart. So often we can easily love others but withhold that love from ourselves. Write yourself the mushiest love letter right now. If you are not sure how to start, consider these suggestions.

- *The top ten things I love about myself are...*

- *I am so proud of myself for...*

- *I deeply care for myself, therefore...*

- *I am amazing at these five things...*

- *I totally deserve love because...*

Get it all on paper right now.

Seeing Through the Eyes of the Heart

Your heart chakra is super savvy about relationships, love, and the interconnectedness of people. Take a moment to tune in to your heart chakra. Start with a few breaths to center, ground, clear, and protect yourself. Now put your hand on your heart chakra and breathe some green light into it. Breathing activates this chakra, so if it's feeling blocked, keep taking deep breaths. Now ask yourself a question about another person or a relationship situation and look through the eyes of your heart and record your results here.

What does your heart tell you about that person or situation?

_____

_____

_____

Can you see what the other person is going through?

_____

_____

_____

What needs to happen to bring love and balance into the picture?

_____

_____

15

The Throat Chakra—
I Speak My Truth

Your throat chakra is all about speaking up, expressing yourself in many ways, and listening to others. It's located right at your throat, and it is a beautiful vibrant blue, like the color of the summer sky. When it's open, we can easily speak up and communicate in all kinds of ways. Any creative expression, like art, poetry, and music, is also a part of this chakra. It is blocked by unspoken words, secrets, and lies or having to keep secrets for others.

It's very difficult to tell the truth, and part of this chakra's psychic powers is in knowing when to be quiet and just listen and also when to speak up and share our truth with others. Our throat chakra also feels the vibration of other people. We sense it in their voices and in their whole being. If you have ever felt like you either "vibed" with someone or not, you were getting psychic information from this chakra.

Finding Your Voice

Take a moment to listen to the sound of your own voice. Maybe even try recording a voice memo on your phone and listening to it. What does your voice sound like?

- ✦ Is it so small and squeaky that you have trouble being heard?

- ✦ Do you feel a lump in your throat and then can't get the words out?

- ✦ Is it loud, clear, and strong?

- ✦ Do you talk a lot but actually say very little?

- ✦ Do you listen well to other people, or are you always talking over people and interrupting?

Which of these statements sounds true for you?

_____

_____

_____

How does it feel to hear your own voice?

_____

_____

_____

Clearing the Throat Chakra

To clear this chakra, we have to make some sounds. Start with taking some breaths to center, ground, clear, and protect yourself. Hover your hand in front of your throat chakra and send some blue light from your hand into the chakra. Now inhale deeply from your toes up your legs and spine and make a noise on the exhale. You can tone an "ahhh" sound, but also open it up to see what kind of voice wants to come out of you. Maybe it's a moan, a groan, a cry, a scream, or a shout of joy. Keep breathing and making sounds until your throat feels loose and clear.

What sounds did you make? Put them in writing here.

_____

_____

_____

_____

What feelings and truths were in those sounds?

_____

_____

_____

_____

_____

Speaking Your Truth

This chakra is blocked by unspoken words and unacknowledged truths. What words have been stuck in your throat, and what do you really need to say right now? Feel free to be really honest; no one will read this but you. Get it all up and out right here.

Sensing the Vibes

The next time you are with someone, tune in to the sound of their voice. Try breathing, swallowing, and opening your jaw a little bit to activate this chakra, and then let yourself experience their vibration. Start by sensing whether the vibe between you is in resonance or not. And then ask your throat chakra to give you any other information about them or the situation and see what happens. Record your experience here.

16

The Brow Chakra—
I See What's Real

Although this is the center of your psychic sight, it is also your mind, your thoughts, how you think, and how you see the world. It's located at your forehead and is an indigo blue, like the midnight sky. When it's open and clear, we see things as they are; we see what's real and true. It is blocked by illusion, and when it's closed, we can't tell what's really going on and we may live more in a fantasy than reality. Learning to notice our thought patterns and beginning to disidentify from our thoughts is the key to clearing this chakra. This is the chakra where clairvoyance happens, and when we clear and open it, we can have more access to this psychic center.

Opening Your Brow Chakra

Meditation is one of the best ways to open this chakra. Try meditating while holding an amethyst crystal. Sandalwood incense or essential oil is also known to open this chakra. Bonus points for chanting the mantra "Om" while you do this! Start by taking a few centering, grounding, and clearing breaths. On the inhale, imagine breathing in indigo-colored light through your brow chakra, filling the center of your head with light. Exhale down your spine into the earth and then repeat this for a few minutes every day.

What happened when you tried this? Document it here.

_____

_____

_____

_____

_____

Did any thoughts or feelings come up?

_____

_____

_____

_____

_____

You might notice more dreams, visions, or other psychic insights directly after this meditation. Record any new insights here.

Clearing Your Brow Chakra

Start with some centering, grounding, and clearing breaths. Place the palm of your hand on your forehead and send some indigo-colored light from your palm into your brow chakra. On the inhale, fill this chakra with light. On the exhale, release anything that is blocking this chakra out your mouth with the breath. Do this when your thoughts are too busy and you are spinning in your mind. It's perfect for right before sleep!

Did you notice a pattern of thoughts that made your mind busy? Journal about what that was like for you here.

Noticing Your Thoughts

Spend some time, an hour maybe, writing down your thoughts as they arise. Even if you only do this for a few minutes, you will be amazed by your own thought patterns.

Are your thoughts repetitive? What are the themes that keep cropping up again and again?

Are your thoughts mostly negative or mostly positive?

Did you notice any thoughts that aren't actually true?

Brow Chakra Meditation for Guidance

Think of a question that you would like some guidance about and write it here.

If you don't have a question, you can just ask yourself, "What do I need to know right now?"

Find somewhere quiet to sit for meditation and start with some basic centering, grounding, and clearing. This time, you are going to breathe indigo light up from your feet, up your spine, to your forehead to open and activate your brow chakra. Now imagine a screen, like a movie or TV screen, appearing in your mind's eye. Ask your question again in your mind and wait to see what images appear on this inner screen. Be open to feeling, knowing, hearing, and messages from your body.

Jot down all that you experienced here.

17

The Crown Chakra—
I Connect with the Divine

The crown chakra creates a connection to the divine as well as universal consciousness and our spirit guides. This chakra is located at the crown of your head, and it seen as either white or a kind of rainbow light that has all the colors in it. When it's open, we feel deep faith and have trust in the great pattern of the universe, even when we can't see what that pattern is in the moment. We believe that it is possible to reach our potential. We have a loving, open, and harmonious connection with the divine source, and we know that this source has our back, no matter what. It is blocked by attachment to the material world, and when it's shut, we feel a lack of faith that can lead to a kind of spiritual hopelessness and despair that is sometimes known as the dark night of the soul. If we are subject to fundamentalist religious beliefs or are not allowed to believe in anything spiritual, this chakra can close up. As we are doing psychic work, it's so important to open up this chakra and keep it open.

Tree of Life Meditation

Start with your centering, grounding, and clearing practice. Sit with a straight back and imagine a big root coming up out of the earth and connecting to your tailbone. Take a deep breath, and on the inhale, pull earth energy up this root, all the way up your spine. Exhale out the top of your head. On each inhale, let the roots go a little deeper. On each exhale, blow this energy out the top of our head and see your crown chakra like the crown of a tree. This opens and clears your crown chakra.

What did you experience when you did this meditation?

_____

_____

_____

_____

Did you have any insights as you did it?

_____

_____

_____

_____

_____

_____

Crown Chakra Affirmations

Try one of these affirmations to open your crown chakra. Say it before you meditate or try it during any psychic work.

- ✦ *I am connected to the universe and am open to receiving messages anytime.*

- ✦ *I trust that the universe always has my back, and I am full of faith.*

- ✦ *I release doubt and attachment and welcome in faith and wisdom.*

- ✦ *I am filled with the pure, radiant light of the divine all the time.*

Jot down one of your own here.

What Do You Believe In?

Exploring your faith can really open up this chakra.

Do you have spiritual beliefs? What do you believe the divine source really is?

_____

_____

_____

_____

_____

_____

Do you believe in angels or other spiritual beings? Write more about that here.

_____

_____

_____

_____

_____

What do you think happens to us when we die, and where do we go?

Do you have wounds that need healing around your religious and spiritual beliefs? What are they?

What do you need to let go of and heal so you can fully open up your crown chakra?

_____

_____

_____

_____

_____

_____

_____

Letter to the Divine/Universe

Have you ever had a conversation with a divine source? It is said that prayer is talking to the divine and meditation is listening, so let's have that conversation right now. Sometimes we need to get some feelings off our chest to open up this chakra. If you are shut down, angry, or sad about your connection to source, it can help to write it all out. Finish the sentence:

Dear Universe (God, Source, or whatever word you use), I really want to tell you...

18

The Magic of Divination

Using divination tools can help us exercise our psychic muscles and give our inner guidance and our spirit guides a way to speak directly to us. A pendulum and an oracle card deck are great places to start. Any oracle deck will do. There are many of them, and it's fun to use your intuition to pick one, or many, for you to use. Get into a habit of daily card pulls and record them in the pages at the back of this journal.

Picking a Card Deck

This can be so much fun! Go into any store that has a lot of oracle card decks. Open up your intuition and ask that you be guided to find the right deck for you. Try holding them to see if you feel a strong pull to one or more of them. You might feel, sense, or know that a specific deck is for you. Let your intuition guide you.

Which one did you pick and why? Journal about the experience here.

Clearing Your Card Deck

When you get a new card deck, it's a good idea to clear the energy from it. Also, if you pull cards regularly, you should clear your deck about once a week or so. Try one of these methods.

- ✦ Use sage or incense to clear your deck. Shuffle the deck and run it through the smoke.

- ✦ Put your deck in a bowl of salt.

- ✦ Place your deck on a sunny windowsill or in the light of the moon.

- ✦ Hold it between your hands and declare that your deck is clear. Tap the deck three times.

Which method did you try, and how did it work for you? Note the results here.

Did you feel a difference in the deck before and after?

The Daily Card Pull

Take a few centering and grounding breaths before you pull your card. Shuffle the deck as you ask a specific question or just ask, "What do I need to know today?" Pull your card in the morning and see how it relates to your day.

Record your card here:

_____

How did your day relate to your card?

_____

_____

_____

_____

_____

_____

_____

_____

Do this every day from now on and record your results in this journal.

Past, Present, Future

Ground and clear yourself and then shuffle your deck. Pull three cards. They can represent the past, present, and future, or they can represent yesterday, today, and tomorrow. Record your cards here.

1. The past: _____

2. The present: _____

3. The future: _____

What does this mean to you, and how does it relate to your life?

_____

_____

_____

_____

_____

_____

_____

_____

_____

Relationship Reading

Ground and clear yourself and then shuffle your deck.

Draw one card to represent yourself and note it down here:

_____

Draw one card to represent the other person:

_____

Draw one card to represent the relationship:

_____

Contemplate what this card spread means to you and journal about it here.

_____

_____

_____

_____

_____

_____

_____

Problem-Solving Card Pull

This is a very useful card spread when you have a problem to solve.

Draw a card to represent the problem or issue and note it down here:

_____

Draw another card for the best outcome and solution for this issue:

_____

Draw a card to show you the action you need to take to get there:

_____

Did this give you any insights on the problem and the solution? Write down your insights here.

_____

_____

_____

_____

_____

_____

Using a Pendulum

You can use almost anything as a pendulum. A needle and thread or the necklace you are already wearing would work just fine, or you can buy a pendulum. Make sure you clear your pendulum and ask it to show you its yes, no, and I-don't-know answers.

Set your elbow on a table and hold the chain or string between your thumb and forefinger. Now ask these questions and record the answers after observing how the pendulum swings.

Show me "yes." What did the pendulum do? Write down or draw the shape here.

Show me "no."

Show me "I don't know."

Pendulum Confirmation

Use your pendulum to confirm or deny any psychic hits and impressions that you might have.

Write down a psychic impression that you have had recently:

_____

_____

_____

_____

_____

_____

Ask your pendulum to confirm whether it was accurate using the yes, no, and I-don't-know pendulum movements. What did the pendulum say?

_____

You can use this method to confirm any psychic hit that you have to help build your confidence and document your results in this journal.

19

Guidance from Within

Getting guidance from our higher self is one of the best sources of psychic information we have. Our intuition is the strongest form of inner guidance that we have. This information comes from our wisest self and is perfect for helping us navigate through life. These practices can help strengthen your inner knowing.

Meet Your Higher Self Meditation

Take a few clearing, grounding, and centering breaths. Imagine that you are somewhere out in nature that appeals to you. Maybe it's a beach, a field of wildflowers, or a mountaintop. Ask that your higher self approach you. Be open to receiving messages from any and all of your psychic senses. Jot down your experiences here.

What does your higher self look like or feel like?

_____

_____

_____

_____

_____

_____

_____

Does your higher self have a name?

_____

_____

What message does your higher self have for you?

Imagine your higher self is giving you a gift, whatever you need most right now. What is it?

Do this meditation regularly to build a connection and relationship with this part of you.

The Soul Mirror

This is a fun way to connect to your higher self. Take a few centering, grounding, clearing breaths. Think about a question or an issue that you would like some guidance about. Or you can ask, "What do I need to know right now?" Look into a mirror and gaze into your own eyes. Keep your breathing relaxed, continue to look into your own eyes, and pay attention to any feelings, thoughts, sensations, or images that arise.

Journal about the experience here.

Crossroads Meditation

This meditation is very helpful when you need to make a decision about something. After doing your centering, grounding, clearing breaths, imagine that you are standing at a crossroads with two or more paths in front of you. Each path represents a possible choice that you can make.

In your mind's eye, look down one possible road. What does that pathway look like and feel like, or what do you sense about it? Is it an easy and fun path, or does it look rocky, steep, or creepy? Describe what that road looks and feels like to you.

_____

_____

_____

_____

If you walked down that path for a while, how does it feel three months into the future?

_____

_____

How about six months from now?

_____

_____

Now examine the other road or roads.

What does this one feel like?

_____

_____

_____

_____

What does it feel like as you walked it into the future?

_____

_____

Come back into the present moment and take some clearing breaths. What does this visualization tell you about what choice to make? Journal about what you learned here.

_____

_____

_____

_____

_____

Your Future Self

Find a quiet place to do some meditation and take a few centering, grounding, and clearing breaths. Now imagine that a version of yourself from ten or twenty years into the future comes to meet you. Note all your observations here by completing the sentences.

My message for you is: _____

_____

_____

You need to be careful of: _____

_____

_____

What you need to do next is: _____

_____

_____

Now do some automatic writing from your future self. Don't overthink it, just start writing here.

_____

_____

_____

Know that you can connect with this part of you anytime you need to.

20

Playing with Nature Spirits

It's super fun and easy to use our connection to nature to increase our psychic abilities. When we are out in nature, we are more naturally grounded, relaxed, and open to receiving psychic messages. Nature spirits are everywhere! And there are many different kinds of them too. They are the spiritual essences of the natural world. *Fairies* are the spirits that inhabit individual plants, and the *elementals* are the spirit essences of water, earth, air, and fire.

Nature spirits love the edges of things, so it's easiest to connect with them at dawn and dusk. They love the edge between the meadow and the forest and the edge between the land and the sea. Make an offering in your garden for them. They respond well to sweet things, like honey, and also to shiny things, and they love music, so wind chimes are also beneficial. It's best to do these practices outside when possible. Relax, enjoy nature, and have some fun with these delightful beings.

Forest Bathing

Find some woods to walk around. If you live in a city, find a park or anywhere there are trees. The deeper into the woods you can go, the better. Just relax and walk through the woods. Take deep breaths and really let the extra oxygen come in. Take a moment to do some grounding and clearing and notice what being in the forest does for your well-being. It's lovely to honor the spirits of the forest in some way. Bring them an offering of cornmeal, tobacco, or something sweet, like honey. Let them know that you want to connect and then sit quietly for a few minutes and see what happens. You might experience things moving out of the corners of your eyes or maybe just feel connected to the web of life around you.

Record your experience here.

Cloud Gazing

I bet you gazed at clouds when you were a child. It's a great way to open up our psychic senses and connect to the spirits of the air. Called *sylphs*, they are spirits of intellect and ideas, and they love wordplay. They love working with people who are journaling! Lie on your back somewhere that you can see the clouds. It's best to do it outside, but you can also look out the window. Relax and do some centering, grounding, and clearing breaths. Go into a relaxed, open, and receptive state and soften the focus of your eyes. You can ask a question or just see what arises in your open, receptive space.

Document your experience here.

Fire Gazing

Gazing like this using the elements is called *scrying*, and it's an ancient and effective technique. Gazing into a fire helps us connect with the elementals of fire, called *salamanders*. They can help us bring about change when we feel stuck and need to connect to what we feel passionately about. You can use any kind of fire, from a fire pit outside to a candle flame. Gaze into the base of the flame where it is hottest and clear and relax your mind. You can ask a question or just be open to receiving any psychic impressions that arise in you.

Write it all down here.

Water Gazing

Gazing into water helps us connect to our emotions and can increase our psychic abilities too. The water elementals are called *undines* and look a bit like mermaids. They inhabit all bodies of water, and it's easiest to connect with them in a natural body of water, like the ocean, a lake, or a river. Sit by the water, ground and clear yourself, and let your gaze relax as you watch the water move. You can also try this with a bowl full of water or even by gazing into your morning tea. It also works well to view the water under the light of the moon. See if you can catch the moonlight in the water to bring extra power to your scrying.

Journal all that you experienced here and don't forget to tune in to all your psychic senses as you do.

Crystal Gazing

The earth element is the hardest to use for scrying because it's so dense and lacks movement. Using crystals is the way around that, and this is the source of the archetype of the fortune-teller gazing into a crystal ball, which really are the best crystals to use for scrying. Scrying works best with quartz crystals and connects us to the earth elementals called *gnomes*. They offer grounding, wisdom, and sometimes the ability to help bring in abundance, just like a leprechaun could help you find a pot of gold. Gnomes have an affinity for treasure, including precious metals and gems.

As you get grounded, cleared, and relaxed, gaze into your crystal and record everything you experience here.

21

Calling All Angels

Angels are wonderful, compassionate beings whose aim is to assistant humanity in our evolution. They offer wonderful healing, guidance, and protection for us. It's important to remember that we need to call them in every day to help us because they can't go against our free will. Here are some beautiful ways to connect with them.

Messages from the Angels

Calling in specific angels is a great way to connect with them, and it's very powerful to work with the archangels. Call on Archangel Michael if you feel that you need protection of any kind. Say out loud, "Archangel Michael, I invoke thee!" And if you have a specific need, say that too. Archangel Raphael is the healer, Gabriel is the archangel of communication, and Ariel is the archangel of love. If you really need help, invoke all four of them, and then wait to see what happens.

Record your experience here.

Ask and You Shall Receive

Try putting your hands on your heart and asking the angels to connect with you. It's wonderful to ask for something very specific, like more strength, courage, or compassion. There are angels called the Virtues who are the divine embodiment of these qualities, and when we ask, they always show up. Look out for signs and omens from them after you ask and record any psychic experiences or signs that happen within the next day or two.

Write it all down here.

22

Connecting with Your Beloveds

Even when someone passes away, their spirit and their love remain connected to us. Learning to contact those who are watching us from heaven can bring us great comfort and ease the difficulties of losing someone. Try these exercises to help you connect to your beloveds who are on the other side.

The Candle Exercise

If you have a picture of your beloved, that is wonderful. Light a white candle, like a tea light, and place it in front of the picture. You can light some incense or sage as well. Do your grounding, clearing, and protecting exercises and then think about what you want to say to your beloved.

Write down a question for them and then pause and breathe. Remain as open and receptive as you can. You might "imagine" what they would say in return. Whatever comes into your mind, write it down here.

Speaking Out Loud

Our loved ones hear us when we speak out loud to them. It's wonderful to have a conversation with someone who has passed. Try it and start by speaking their name out loud first. This acts as a kind of invocation. Then say what you want to say and know they are hearing you. When you are done, ask them to send you a sign that they heard you and watch for signs for the next few days. Record any you noticed here.

23

More Practices

These are some fun exercises to do either
by yourself or with a partner.

Counting Cars

This one is fun to do with a friend. You can do this anywhere you can see a slow flow of traffic passing by. Center, ground, and clear yourself and set your intention to turn your psychic abilities on. Relax your mind and slow your breathing with the intention of creating an open and receptive state of psychic awareness. See if you can predict what the color of the next car coming will be and record the experiment here. You will be surprised by how accurate you can become with this.

1. _____

2. _____

3. _____

4. _____

5. _____

Holding a Card

Take one of your oracle card decks or use a playing card deck. Shuffle the deck, and without looking at the card, hold it in your hand. Prep yourself by doing some centering, grounding, and clearing and then relax into a state of open receptivity. Can you sense anything about the card? Record any images, colors, feelings, or messages you receive and write them down here. Then look at the card and see how what you experienced relates to the card.

Sensing Someone's Aura

Get yourself grounded and receptive, and then with someone's permission, try reading their aura. This works best if they are in front of a white wall. Look at them with a soft focus and out of the corner of your eye. You might see colors or a glow of light. Try closing your eyes and "looking" again. Ask yourself the question, *What can I perceive about their aura?* and open up all your psychic senses. You might feel, sense, or hear the answer; feel something in your body; or see something in your mind's eye. Jot down what you experienced here.

Recording Your Psychic Experiences

Now that you are in the swing of recording your psychic experiences, I want to encourage you to continue to record them on your own. This is the best thing you can do to continue to strengthen your psychic muscles and awaken your psychic abilities. By now, you have created a beautiful habit that I highly encourage you to continue. Don't stop now!

To that end, here is an example of a week's worth of space to record your own experiences. Use these categories to document your continuing psychic experiences, so every time you have a dream or experience an omen, you record it here, in the following pages.

I enthusiastically recommend that you then carry on this practice as a regular part of your life. It's something that I still do in my daily life, and I reap enormous benefits, insights, and wisdom. I want that for you too.

Here are some of the categories of experiences you can record on the following pages.

DREAM IMAGES

Keep this journal by your bed and record any dreams you have had before you even get out of bed. Start with snippets of images, emotions, and feelings about your dreams, and before you know it, you will be remembering them all.

DAILY CARD PULLS

Adding daily card pulls from your decks is a powerful way to develop your psychic muscles and gain the daily wisdom you need to live your life in the flow of your own inner guidance. Pull from the oracle card decks you are using, record the results here, along with your interpretation of what they mean for you, and watch your access to your inner wisdom grow.

HUNCHES, NUDGES, INTUITIVE HITS

Oftentimes our psychic impressions come in the form of hunches, inner nudges, and intuitive insights called psychic hits. Use this section to record any of those experiences and any other aha moments. If you write them down here, you can claim psychic brownie points when your predictions come to pass.

SIGNS AND OMENS

Our world is rich with signs and omens from the spirit world, and when we are tuned in to these "winks from the universe," we can use them as confirmation that we are receiving the right messages and heading on the right path. They might be repeating numbers, messages in music, the things other people say, or what is happening in nature around you. You will know it by the special feeling these events have, and you will definitely get more of them if you pay attention to them and honor the moments by recording them here.

FIRST IMPRESSIONS

Paying attention to and recording your first impressions are wonderful ways to increase your psychic discernment—that is, the ability to tell what's really going on and to see underneath the surface of things to find the truth. Our first impressions of people, places, and situations are usually right, and by documenting them, we can increase our ability to practice discernment on all levels of our being. Record them all here.

SPIRIT PRESENCES

Spirits are all around us! You can definitely learn to sense the presence of your angels, your beloved ancestor spirits, and even the wandering spirits that are just passing through. Remember to open up to all your psychic senses because you might see, feel, sense, hear, or know about the presence of a spirit being. Whenever you sense one, document it here, and you can also use your pendulum to help you know who or what you are sensing if you are not sure.

Of course, you can also just let your intuition guide you and simply start writing to see what happens. Continuing this practice will keep your psychic and intuitive flow going and expanding. Don't forget, your psychic abilities are a lot like muscles, and the more often you give them some loving and gentle exercise, the more they grow.

DREAM IMAGES

_____
_____
_____
_____
_____

DAILY CARD PULLS

_____
_____
_____
_____
_____

HUNCHES, NUDGES, INTUITIVE HITS

_____
_____
_____
_____
_____

SIGNS AND OMENS

_____

_____

_____

_____

_____

FIRST IMPRESSIONS

_____

_____

_____

_____

_____

SPIRIT PRESENCES

_____

_____

_____

_____

_____

Date: _____

DREAM IMAGES

_____
_____
_____
_____
_____

DAILY CARD PULLS

_____
_____
_____
_____
_____

HUNCHES, NUDGES, INTUITIVE HITS

_____
_____
_____
_____
_____

SIGNS AND OMENS

FIRST IMPRESSIONS

SPIRIT PRESENCES

DREAM IMAGES

_____

_____

_____

_____

_____

DAILY CARD PULLS

_____

_____

_____

_____

_____

HUNCHES, NUDGES, INTUITIVE HITS

_____

_____

_____

_____

_____

SIGNS AND OMENS

_____

_____

_____

_____

FIRST IMPRESSIONS

_____

_____

_____

_____

SPIRIT PRESENCES

_____

_____

_____

_____

Date: _____

DREAM IMAGES

_____
_____
_____
_____
_____

DAILY CARD PULLS

_____
_____
_____
_____
_____

HUNCHES, NUDGES, INTUITIVE HITS

_____
_____
_____
_____
_____

SIGNS AND OMENS

FIRST IMPRESSIONS

SPIRIT PRESENCES

DREAM IMAGES

_____

_____

_____

_____

_____

DAILY CARD PULLS

_____

_____

_____

_____

HUNCHES. NUDGES. INTUITIVE HITS

_____

_____

_____

_____

SIGNS AND OMENS

FIRST IMPRESSIONS

SPIRIT PRESENCES

DREAM IMAGES

_____

_____

_____

_____

_____

DAILY CARD PULLS

_____

_____

_____

_____

_____

HUNCHES, NUDGES, INTUITIVE HITS

_____

_____

_____

_____

_____

SIGNS AND OMENS

FIRST IMPRESSIONS

SPIRIT PRESENCES

DREAM IMAGES

_____
_____
_____
_____
_____

DAILY CARD PULLS

_____
_____
_____
_____
_____

HUNCHES, NUDGES, INTUITIVE HITS

_____
_____
_____
_____
_____

SIGNS AND OMENS

_____

_____

_____

_____

FIRST IMPRESSIONS

_____

_____

_____

_____

SPIRIT PRESENCES

_____

_____

_____

_____

Lisa Campion is a psychic counselor and Reiki master teacher with more than twenty-five years of experience. She has trained more than one thousand practitioners in the hands-on, energy-healing practice of Reiki, including medical professionals; and has conducted more than fifteen thousand individual sessions in her career. Campion is author of several books, including *The Art of Psychic Reiki*. Based near Providence, RI; she specializes in training emerging psychics, empaths, and healers so they can fully step into their gifts—the world needs all the healers it can get!

More Books from Energy Healer & Psychic Trainer Lisa Campion

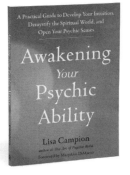

This transformative guide will help you develop and harness your own psychic ability, so you can live your life with a greater sense of meaning and purpose.

ISBN 978-1648480744 / US $19.95

This healing guide will help you cultivate energy management skills to cope with energy vampires and narcissists, increase your own vitality, and embrace your unique gifts.

ISBN 978-1684035922 / US $18.95

This step-by-step guide will teach you the sacred art of Reiki while cultivating the psychic and intuitive skills crucial to this healing energy work.

ISBN 978-1684031214 / US $19.95

REVEAL PRESS

newharbingerpublications

1-800-748-6273 / newharbinger.com